◧ READERS

Pre-level 1

Fishy Tales
Colorful Days
Garden Friends
Party Fun
In the Park
Farm Animals
Petting Zoo
Let's Make Music
Meet the Dinosaurs
Duck Pond Dip
My Dress-up Box
On the Move

Snakes Slither and Hiss
Family Vacation
Ponies and Horses
My Day
Monkeys
John Deere: Busy Tractors
LEGO® DUPLO®: On the Farm
Cuentos de Peces *en español*
Dias Ilenos de color *en español*
Star Wars: Blast Off!
Star Wars The Clone Wars: Don't Wake the
   Zillo Beast!

Level 1

A Day at Greenhill Farm
Truck Trouble
Tale of a Tadpole
Surprise Puppy!
Duckling Days
A Day at Seagull Beach
Whatever the Weather
Busy Buzzy Bee
Big Machines
Wild Baby Animals
A Bed for the Winter
Born to be a Butterfly
Dinosaur's Day
Feeding Time
Diving Dolphin
Rockets and Spaceships
My Cat's Secret
First Day at Gymnastics
A Trip to the Zoo
I Can Swim!
A Trip to the Library
A Trip to the Doctor
A Trip to the Dentist
I Want to be a Ballerina
Animal Hide and Seek
Submarines and Submersibles
Animals at Home
Let's Play Soccer
Homes Around the World
Bugs and Us

LEGO® DUPLO®: Around Town
LEGO® City: Trouble at the Bridge
LEGO® City: Secret at Dolphin Bay
LEGO® Pirates: Blackbeard's Treasure
Star Wars: What is a Wookiee?
Star Wars: Ready, Set, Podrace!
Star Wars: Luke Skywalker's Amazing Story
Star Wars: Tatooine Adventures
Star Wars: Who Saved the Galaxy?
Star Wars The Clone Wars: Watch Out for
   Jabba the Hutt!
Star Wars The Clone Wars: Pirates... and
   Worse
Indiana Jones: Indy's Adventures
John Deere: Good Morning, Farm!
A Day in the Life of a Builder
A Day in the Life of a Dancer
A Day in the Life of a Firefighter
A Day in the Life of a Teacher
A Day in the Life of a Musician
A Day in the Life of a Doctor
A Day in the Life of a Police Officer
A Day in the Life of a TV Reporter
Gigantes de Hierro *en español*
Crías del mundo animal *en español*

A Note to Parents

DK READERS is a compelling program for beginning readers, designed in conjunction with leading literacy experts, including Dr. Linda Gambrell, Distinguished Professor of Education at Clemson University. Dr. Gambrell has served as President of the National Reading Conference, the College Reading Association, and the International Reading Association.

Beautiful illustrations and superb full-color photographs combine with engaging, easy-to-read stories to offer a fresh approach to each subject in the series. Each DK READER is guaranteed to capture a child's interest while developing his or her reading skills, general knowledge, and love of reading.

The five levels of DK READERS are aimed at different reading abilities, enabling you to choose the books that are exactly right for your child:

Pre-level 1: Learning to read
Level 1: Beginning to read
Level 2: Beginning to read alone
Level 3: Reading alone
Level 4: Proficient readers

The "normal" age at which a child begins to read can be anywhere from three to eight years old. Adult participation through the lower levels is very helpful for providing encouragement, discussing storylines, and sounding out unfamiliar words.

No matter which level you select, you can be sure that you are helping your child learn to read, then read to learn!

LONDON, NEW YORK, MUNICH,
MELBOURNE, AND DELHI

Editor Pamela Afram
Project Art Editor Clive Savage
Managing Editor Laura Gilbert
Design Manager Maxine Pedliham
Art Director Ron Stobbart
Publisher Simon Beecroft
Publishing Director Alex Allan
Pre-Production Producer Rebecca Fallowfield
Senior Producer Shabana Shakir
Jacket Designer Satvir Sihota

Designed and edited by Tall Tree Ltd
Designer Malcolm Parchment
Editor Jon Richards

Reading Consultant Linda B. Gambrell, Ph.D.

For Lucasfilm
Executive Editor Jonathan W. Rinzler
Art Director Troy Alders
Keeper of the Holocron Leland Chee
Director of Publishing Carol Roeder

First American Edition, 2013
10 9 8 7 6 5 4 3 2 1
Published in the United States by DK Publishing
375 Hudson Street, New York, New York 10014

DK books are available at special discounts when purchased in bulk
for sales promotions, premiums, fund-raising, or educational use.
For details, contact:
DK Publishing Special Markets
375 Hudson Street, New York, New York 10014
SpecialSales@dk.com

A catalog record for this book is available
from the Library of Congress.

ISBN: 978-1-4654-0585-2 (Paperback)
ISBN: 978-1-4654-0586-9 (Hardcover)

Color reproduction by Alta Image
Printed and bound in China by L.Rex

Discover more at
www.dk.com
www.starwars.com

Contents

4 Introduction

6 The Jedi

8 Yoda

10 Anakin
   Skywalker

12 Mace Windu

14 Quinlan Vos

16 Obi-Wan
   Kenobi

18 Ahsoka Tano

20 Tera Sinube

22 The Sith

24 Darth Sidious

26 Count Dooku

28 Asajj Ventress

30 Masters of the
   Force

32 Glossary

DK READERS

LEARNING TO READ — pre-level 1

STAR WARS

THE CLONE WARS

Masters of the Force

Written by Jon Richards

These warriors are
Masters of the Force.
They use a special
power called the Force.

The Force makes them
very strong fighters.
It also gives them
special talents.

Masters of the Force can be good or bad.

Obi-Wan
Kenobi

Mace
Windu

The good ones are
called the Jedi.

Ahsoka Tano

Anakin
Skywalker

Yoda

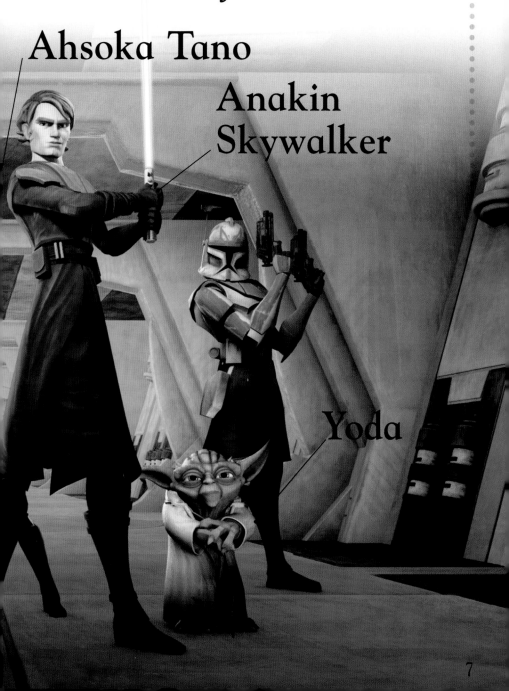

This is Jedi
Grand Master Yoda.
He is using the Force
to fight battle droids.

Yoda (YOH-DAH)

_____ lightsaber

This is Jedi Knight Anakin Skywalker.

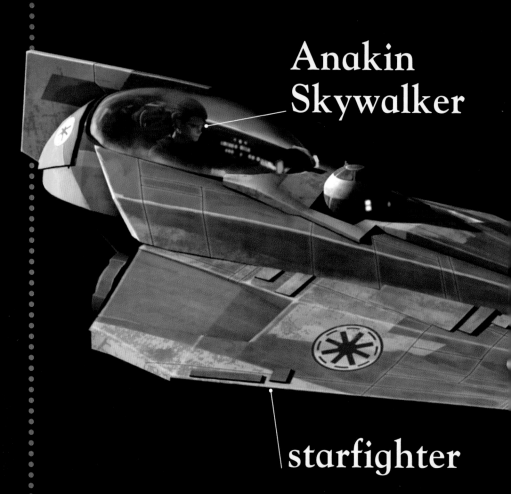

Anakin Skywalker

\starfighter

Anakin Skywalker
(AN-A-KIN SKY-WAH-KER)

He is using the Force
to fly a starfighter
with amazing skill.

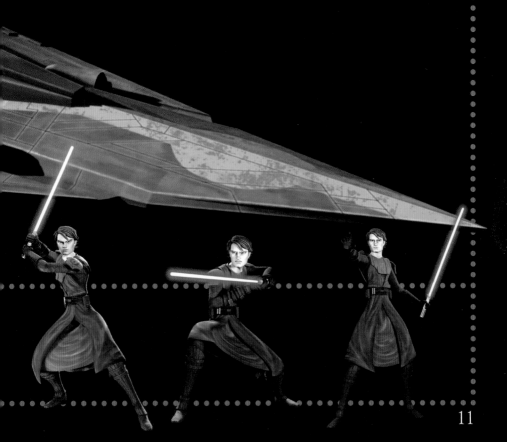

This is Jedi Master
Mace Windu.

clone trooper

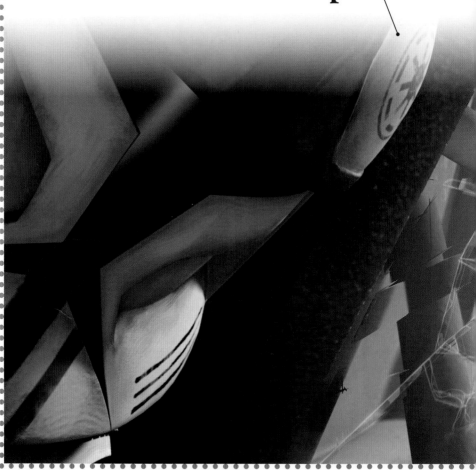

Mace Windu
(MAYSS WIN-DOO)

He is using the Force
to shatter a windshield
to save a clone trooper.

gunship

Quinlan Vos
(QWIN-LAN VOS)

This is Jedi Master
Quinlan Vos.
He is using the Force
to jump from a gunship.

This is Jedi general Obi-Wan Kenobi.

clone
trooper

Obi-Wan Kenobi
(OH-BEE WON KE-NOH-BEE)

He is using the Force
to lead clone troopers
in battle.

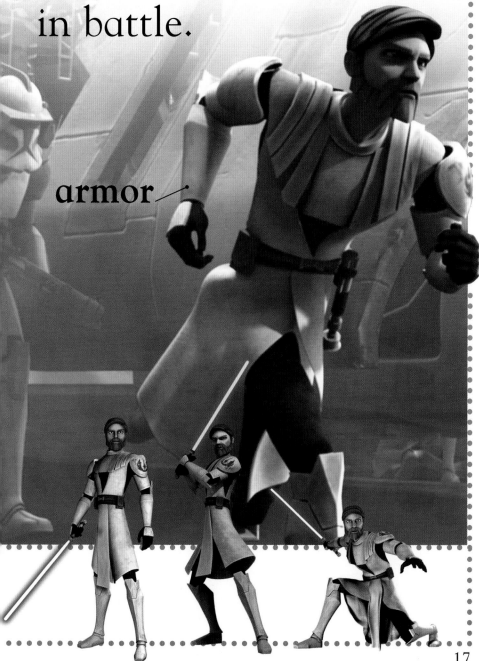

armor

This is Jedi Padawan
Ahsoka Tano.

She is using the Force
to push commando
droids away from her.

Ahsoka Tano
(AH-SOH-KAR TAR-NOH)

commando
droid

This is Jedi Master
Tera Sinube.

lightsaber

Tera Sinube
(TE-RAR SY-NOO-BEE)

He is using the Force to fight a criminal.

Not everyone uses the Force for good, like the Jedi.

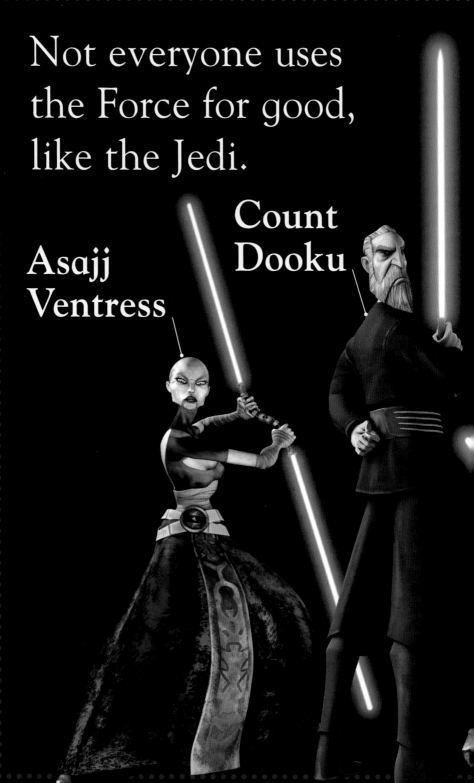

Asajj
Ventress

Count
Dooku

Some use the Force
for evil.
They are called
the Sith.

Darth
Maul

Savage
Opress

Darth Sidious is the strongest Sith.

Darth Sidious
(DARTH SID-EE-US)

He is using the Force
to shoot lightning
at his enemies.

This is evil Sith
Count Dooku.

Count Dooku
(COUNT DOO-KOO)

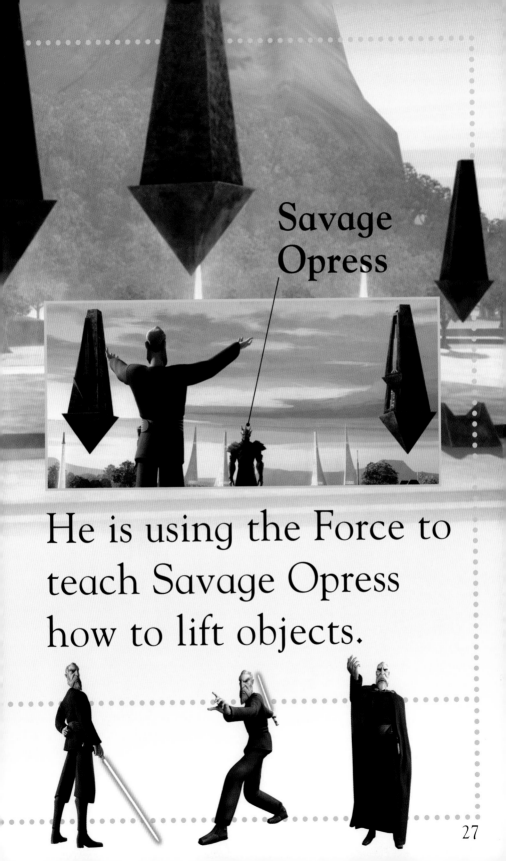

Savage
Opress

He is using the Force to
teach Savage Opress
how to lift objects.

Ventress fights for the Sith.

Ventress
(VEN-TRESS)

She is using
the Force
to choke
her victims.

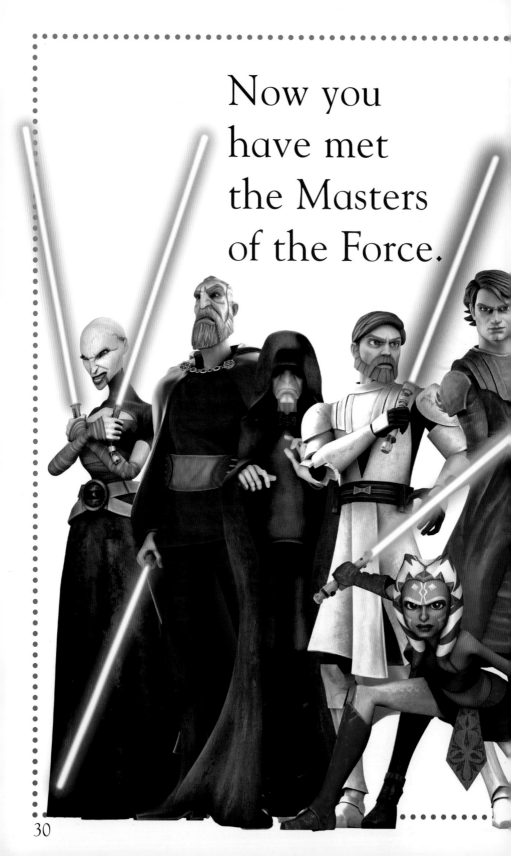

Now you
have met
the Masters
of the Force.

Who do you think is the most powerful?

Glossary

Clone troopers
A group of soldiers who are the same as each other.

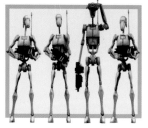

Commando droid
A robot that is built to fight in wars.

Gunship
A large aircraft with lots of weapons.

Lightsaber
A special sword used by the Jedi and the Sith.

Starfighter
A small spacecraft that is used in battles.

Index

Amidala, Padmé 26

battle droids 7, 15, 25

Chewbacca 29

cyborg 24, 25

Force 13

Grievous, General 24–25

head-tails 4

Jedi 5, 6, 7, 8, 18, 20, 30

Kiros 18

Mon Cala 18

Padawan 8

lightsaber 8, 9, 15, 23, 25

Rotta the Huttlet 26, 27

Shili 4

Sith 7, 20

Skywalker, Anakin 6, 9, 11

speeder bike 18

starfighter 16, 17

Togruta 4

Trandoshans 29

Unduli, Luminara 6, 7

Ventress. Asajj 6, 7, 23

Wookiee 29

Yoda 6

E RICHA   BLU
Richards, Jon.
Star Wars, the clone wars.

BLUE RIDGE
01/14